T0013603

★ ★ ★ ★ ★ ★ ★ THE ★ ★ ★ ★ ★ ★ ★
SECRET SOLDIER
★ ★ ★ ★ ★ ★ ★ ★ ★ ★ ★ ★ ★ ★ ★ ★ ★ ★

The Story of Deborah Sampson

By Ann McGovern

Illustrated by Harold Goodwin
Cover illustration by Katherine Thompson

ISBN 978-0-590-43052-4

66   22/0

Printed in the U.S.A.   40

SCHOLASTIC INC.
New York Toronto London Auckland
Sydney Mexico City New Delhi Hong Kong

Sent Away

Deborah's mother looked down at her five sleeping children. She had not slept all night.

In a few hours the sun would come up. It would be a new day — the terrible day she would have to give her children away.

Deborah's father had left home to sail the seas in search of adventure. Now he was dead, drowned in a shipwreck at sea.

Deborah's mother was sick and poor. She could no longer take care of all her little ones.

She touched the sleeping children, one by one. Her hand stayed the longest on Deborah's soft, brown hair.

"You are most like your father," she thought. "It is you I will miss the most."

Deborah Sampson was only five years old when she had to leave her mother and her home in Plympton, Massachusetts. It was the year 1765, ten years before the start of the Revolutionary War.

She was sent to live with Miss Fuller, her mother's cousin.

Cousin Fuller was sweet and jolly. She never had children of her own. But she knew just what would make a sad little girl happy again.

She baked cookies for Deborah. She gave Deborah a bed of her own — a soft feather bed that she did not have to share with anyone.

Deborah loved her kind cousin.

Miss Fuller taught her how to spin and weave, and how to make bread.

But best of all were the wonderful hours of reading lessons.

Deborah learned the alphabet by heart. She learned to read quickly.

For three years Deborah was happy.

Then one day Miss Fuller became ill. Three days later she was dead. Deborah cried. Dear, sweet Cousin Fuller. She had been like a mother to Deborah.

Deborah was now eight years old and without a home. Her own mother was still too sick to take care of her. She tried to find another place for Deborah to live.

The only person who would take Deborah in was 80-year-old Mrs. Thatcher, who lived in Middleborough.

Mrs. Thatcher must be the oldest lady in the world, Deborah thought.

Mrs. Thatcher was too feeble to do anything for herself. Deborah had to do everything. She had to feed old Mrs. Thatcher like a baby. The old lady could hardly lift her spoon to her mouth.

Deborah did all the hard work too. She carried in heavy loads of wood for the fire. She kept the fire going and swept up the ashes. She washed the clothes and did all of the cooking.

Every day was like every other — full of hard work and loneliness.

It was too much for an eight-year-old girl.

But there was nothing else Deborah could do. That's how it was for a poor girl without anyone to take care of her.

"If only I could see my mother," Deborah thought over and over.

But her mother lived too far away and besides, who would take Deborah there?

Sometimes Deborah thought she did not have a friend in all the world.

She was wrong.

The minister of Middleborough thought about Deborah often. He came to see how she was getting on.

He saw the feeble old lady nodding her head by the fire. He saw Deborah growing taller — and thinner — and paler.

The good minister made a promise to himself. "I will get this child out of here," he said.

He kept his promise.

Mrs. Thatcher was sent to live with relatives. And Deborah was sent to live with Deacon Thomas and his family in the same town of Middleborough.

A Family Again

A family! A laughing, loving, crying, hugging family! Deborah had almost forgotten what a family was.

But the Thomas family was not *her* family. She knew what she was in the Thomas household. A servant. And she knew she would have to be a servant for 10 years. That was the agreement. Deacon Thomas would give her a place to stay, food to eat, and clothes to wear. Deborah knew she would have to work hard for 10 years.

Ten years. A long time.

"What will I be like in 10 years?" she wondered. Ten years from now was too far away to think about. Better think about right now. At least she had her own little room, above the kitchen, in the loft upstairs.

And there was plenty to do right now. Mrs. Thomas had four lively little boys for her to look after. She dressed the youngest, fed them, and told them stories. She helped with every job in the house and in the barn. She swept, cleaned, cooked, carried in the wood, and brought in the water.

But the family was so lively and Deborah was kept so busy that she soon forgot the lonely, long days at Mrs. Thatcher's house.

There was so much to do, Deborah hardly had a moment to herself. She had no time to do what she liked best — reading.

In those days, people did not think it was important for girls to read. Some people thought too much reading gave girls brain fever.

Deacon Thomas and his wife thought all a girl had to learn was how to work well.

Deborah was a good worker. She grew strong as she milked the cows, fed the pigs, and tended the chickens. She learned how to harness the family horse, and she rode the horse to the village on errands.

She helped plow the fields. When it looked like rain, she raked up all the hay and stored it neatly inside the barn. She learned how to make the things she needed — a basket, a sled, a milking stool.

Deborah taught the three oldest boys how to read. So when summer came, they were ready to go to the summer school in the village.

School started at 6:30 in the morning and lasted two and half hours. Then the boys came home to do their share of work. Late in the afternoon they went back to school.

Deborah would stand at the window and watch the boys run laughing down the road.

"If only I could go with them," she thought.

When the boys came home, she begged them to teach her what they had learned that day. But they didn't want to talk about school or learning. They only wanted to wrestle with her and tease her.

The Thomas children thought Deborah was odd, even a little crazy. Why did she care so much about school? Why did she ask so many questions?

How do flowers and vegetables grow, and why?

What are the stars made of? How far away are they?

What makes the sun set and the moon rise?

Deborah often got up before the sun rose and climbed to the top of a nearby hill to watch the night sky lighten into day.

Deborah begged Deacon Thomas to let her go to school sometimes. But there was always too much work to do.

There was a new baby in the house now and another on the way. She couldn't be spared.

So Deborah borrowed the children's school books. At night, in her little room above the kitchen, she read until her candle flickered out.

She practiced writing with a pen she made herself from goose feathers. She dipped the pen into homemade ink and wrote on a piece of bark from a birch tree.

She started writing in a diary — a book in which she wrote down her good and her bad thoughts and deeds.

On the right-hand pages she wrote down all of her good thoughts and the good things she had done.

On the left-hand pages she wrote down all the things she thought of as bad. The left-hand pages filled up first.

Deacon Thomas had to say to her often, "I wish you wouldn't spend so much time scribbling."

There was one lesson Deacon Thomas thought all his children should learn — how to use money wisely. Every child in the family was given some lambs to raise and sell. They were allowed to keep the money to buy something useful.

Deacon Thomas let Deborah have some lambs too. She took good care of her flock and got a good price for them.

It was the first time she ever had money of her own. She had earned it herself. It was a good feeling. Carefully, she wrapped the money in a handkerchief and put it away.

A Country in Trouble

The America of Deborah Sampson's time was nothing like the America of today, with its millions of people living in 50 states.

Most of the country was still wilderness, where Indians lived.

People had come from across the ocean and settled in colonies along the Eastern coast. Deborah was born in the Massachusetts Bay Colony. There were 13 colonies. Most of the people who settled there were English and all of the

13 colonies belonged to England. The people were ruled by the King of England far across the sea.

In time, many people in the 13 colonies wanted to be free from English rule. They wanted to make their own laws.

But the King of England wanted to keep his colonies. He needed money for his government. One way to get money from the colonies was to make the people pay taxes.

Most of the people in the colonies did not think that was fair. The King made rules about many things the people did not think were fair — rules about hunting and farming and fishing. Rules about running their business and even rules about worshipping God.

Year after year, the trouble between the colonies and England got worse.

In every village, on every farm, the people talked about the troubles.

Should America be free from England? they asked. Even if it meant war?

Like everyone else, Deborah Sampson heard about the troubles too.

1770   Deborah was 10 years old.

In Boston, the people were angry. The King of England had sent over his red-coated soldiers to see that his rules were carried out. The Americans didn't want the soldiers there in the first place. And then they heard they would have to pay for the soldiers' expenses.

1773   Deborah was 13 years old.

Although most Americans loved to drink tea, they said they would not buy all their tea from England. They wanted to be free to buy tea from any country they chose.

But England sent over ships loaded with tea anyway. One night in Boston, some Americans dressed up as Indians.

They went aboard the three English
ships in the harbor and they dumped all
that tea into the water.

Deborah heard about the Boston Tea
Party, and laughed. But when the Eng-
lish King heard about it, he was furious.
He sent over more red-coated soldiers.

1774 Deborah was 14 years old.

The King punished the people of
Boston. He said no ships could sail in or
out of Boston until the tea was paid for.

Everyone worried that the people of
Boston would starve. They thought of

ways to help them. Some people planted extra corn to send to the hungry people of Boston. Deborah helped plant the corn on the Thomas farm.

1775   Deborah was 15.

The trouble was getting worse. In many villages, people were getting ready for war. Groups of men and young boys began training to be soldiers. They were called minutemen because they were ready to fight at a minute's notice.

Deborah watched them drill in her village.

People in many villages began to collect guns and barrels of powder. They hid them in secret places.

One night, the British soldiers were sent to the town of Concord, near Boston, to seize the hidden guns and powder.

But some colonists found out where the British soldiers were going. The people had to be warned! The minute-men had to be called out!

That night Paul Revere and William Dawes rode their horses on the roads to Lexington and Concord, warning the people, "The British are coming."

So by the time the British soldiers reached the town of Lexington, near Concord, they found more than 50 minutemen ready for them.

The fight that followed was the first of the Revolutionary War.

Deborah heard the bells of Middleborough ringing, marking that first battle of the long war ahead.

1776 Deborah was 16.

A brave farmer from Virginia had been chosen to lead the American army. His name was George Washington.

In the city of Philadelphia, an important paper was being read before the first Congress. That paper was the Declaration of Independence. It said that all men were created equal. And it said that they have the right to form their own government, to be a free country — free from England's rule.

On July 4, 1776, the people in Congress voted for the Declaration of Independence — they voted to be the United States of America. News of the new government reached across the land. Deborah heard the bells of Middleborough ring out again.

But not everyone in the colonies wanted the new United States. Some people still wanted to belong to England. They were still loyal to the English king. These people were called *Tories.*

It was one thing for America to say it was free. But it was another thing to win freedom!

1778 Deborah was 18.

The war was long. The news was sad. So many times it seemed that the United States was losing the war.

Then help came from France. Ships and soldiers came from France to help the weary American soldiers.

France helped America win some of the important battles that would put an end to the long, long war.

The Thomas children were growing up. Deborah said good-bye to the oldest boy who left home and went to war.

Free – to Do What?

Year by year, the United States was growing closer to the time when it could stand alone.

And year by year, Deborah was growing closer to her independence too — the time she could go out into the world and be on her own.

At last Deborah was 18 years old. It was the year 1778 and she was free!

But free to do what? She was a woman. That meant she could not learn a trade, the way young men did.

The Thomas family still needed Deborah's help around the house and farm. They asked her to stay on for the winter.

It was her first winter of freedom, but she spent it doing the same kind of work she had done for the past ten years.

In the summertime she left the Thomas house.

She was going to be a schoolteacher! She—Deborah Sampson—who had never even been to school as a pupil was going to teach in the town school.

It was because of the war. Every man who could have taught in the summer school was busy with the war. There was no one left to teach.

Some people knew that Deborah had taught reading and writing to the Thomas children.

She might work out, they thought.

Hope and fear were all mixed up in Deborah when she left the Thomas house. She took a room in the house next door to the school in the village.

The school was the same as other schools of New England. There were a few books — the *New England Primer* and a spelling book and a few bibles.

There were a few girls in her class of 20 pupils. She remembered how she would have given almost anything to be able to go to school and learn when she

was young. So although she was supposed to teach the girls only sewing and knitting, and how to read a little, she taught them everything she knew. She taught them spelling and writing and everything she had read about stars and rivers and mountains.

How proud she was at the end of the summer when she was asked to come back the next year.

But what could she do all those months until next summer came?

Maybe her mother would have an idea. Deborah went to visit her.

Deborah's mother worried about her.

"Why aren't you thinking about getting married, child, like girls are supposed to do?" her mother asked.

In those days girls were expected to get married as soon as they could. Then they were expected to begin to raise a big family.

Deborah loved children, but she wanted

to do other things — daring things — before she married and settled down.

In those days, married women had very few rights. A married woman could not have a house or a farm or money of her own. The law said everything she had belonged to her husband. She could not own anything. The husband had the right to make the decisions about everything — even what happened to the children.

No, Deborah was in no hurry to get married.

Deborah dreamed of a great adventure. Doing housework from morning till night and looking after a house full of babies was not her idea of a great adventure. Not yet. Not now.

Now she wanted to travel, to walk in different places, to see different faces.

During the war she had heard of Boston, Philadelphia, New York. Would she ever see those great cities?

In those days, if a poor man wanted to travel and have adventures, he joined the army.

"Why can't I join the army too?" Deborah thought. Then she laughed at herself.

"Me — Deborah Sampson — a soldier!" she thought. She knew the army was only for men.

"Wait," she told herself. "Why not me? Wasn't I a teacher without ever going to school? Wasn't I a *good* teacher?

Why not a soldier? Why not dress like a man and be a soldier!"

She went to sleep that night thinking about it. She dreamed about it.

And when she woke up, her head was filled with the single thought. It wasn't a dream now. It was a hope — a plan — a secret plan!

That winter she worked as a weaver. She lived in one home for weeks at a time while she wove clothes for the family. Then she moved on to another home.

She was weaving cloth, but she was also weaving plans. She told no one about them. There was no one to share her secret with, no one to give her advice.

Her plans grew sharper in her mind.

She had some money, wrapped in a handkerchief, that first money she had earned from selling her sheep long ago.

But she would need more money. She would have to get new clothes — men's clothes.

The Fortune Teller

When Deborah was 21, the Americans won an important battle at Yorktown, Virginia. But the fighting was not yet over.

America had a big problem with Tories. Tories were people who lived in America but who believed America should still be ruled by England. Tories did not want America to be a free and independent country.

Often the Tories would steal food and guns from the Americans and give them to the British soldiers. Often the Tories and the Americans fought each other.

By now the people were getting tired of fighting. The war had been dragging on for six years.

General Washington began calling for a different kind of soldier. He did not want the old kind of fighting men — the men who would stay in the army for only a few months and then go back to their farms.

He wanted soldiers to sign up for the army for three years at a time. Continental soldiers, they were called.

Many men were answering the call and signing up for three years.

Deborah was getting more and more restless.

She would do one more weaving job.

She wove cloth to tie around her chest so she would look flat-chested, like a boy. She wove a piece of cloth big enough to make a man's suit of clothes for herself. She bought a man's hat and shoes.

One day she put on all her clothes for the first time.

"Do I still look like me?" she wondered. "Would my mother know me?"

She would make another trip to her mother. It would be a test!

She passed it. Her own mother did not know her.

A fortune-teller lived near her mother's house. Deborah, wearing her man's disguise, went to see him.

"I am not here to take your advice," she said in the deepest voice she could manage. "I am only curious as to what you will say to me."

"You are an honest man," the fortune-teller told Deborah. "I see in your future many adventures. But not all of them will be successful."

Deborah's Secret Plan

Deborah's mind was made up. She would go to Boston and enlist in the army.

But she would wait a while longer. The weather in March was cold and stormy. She would have to travel alone through deep snows and in winds that could knock her down.

She would wait for spring.

Deborah used her free time getting used to acting like a man. When no one was looking, she put on her strange clothes. She practiced sitting and standing and walking and running and speaking in a deep voice.

The weather became warmer. The melting snows dripped down from the great pine trees. Birds sang, and a young man fell in love with Deborah.

Deborah's mother could not see why her daughter did not like him.

"He is a lump of a man," Deborah told her mother. "That's why."

One day he came to see Deborah. He was drunk. He had been drinking too much rum. Deborah wrote in her diary: "From that day on, I set him down a fool."

Deborah was ready to set her secret plan into action.

She went to bed at her regular bedtime. She slept for a few hours and woke at midnight. Deborah put on her man's clothes. She set off for the town of Taunton, 10 miles away. She walked all night. The next morning she saw her old neighbor, William Bennett, walking toward her. Her eyes met his and she jumped. Did he know her? Her heart pounded like a drum. Could he hear it? Surely she would be followed, she thought.

She made for the woods. She sat under a big pine tree. She had been walking for such a long time. She was so tired. Soon she was fast asleep.

It was dark when she woke up. Where was the road? At last she found it. Again she walked all night. She walked and she walked — and she found herself back in her old neighborhood!

"Give up!" one part of her cried. "You can't do it. Stay home where you belong!"

"Go on!" another part of her cried. "You can do it. Think of the adventures. You want to see rivers and mountains and cities. You want to see Boston."

She went on to Boston, walking all the way.

Deborah thought Boston must be the biggest city in the world. She had never seen that many people before in one place. Or that many houses. Or streets. Or horses and carriages. Or soldiers. . .

Deborah was hungry. She didn't have any money left, not even a penny for bread. It was time for the next part of her plan.

They Call Her "Bobby"

On May 20, 1782, Deborah Sampson joined the army as a Continental soldier. She said her name was Robert Shurtliff.

"We'll put you down for three years, if the war lasts that long," she was told as she signed her strange new name.

At first she was afraid to open her mouth to speak, afraid that she could not keep her voice deep enough.

At first she was afraid someone would find out she was a woman by the way she sat or walked or shook hands.

But wonder of wonders — no one guessed who she really was!

They thought she was young — 15 years old — because she had no beard. Most of the time the men called her Bobby. But sometimes, to tease her, they called her "Blooming Boy."

Her first test as a soldier was a hard one. She had to make a long march to West Point in New York.

She marched with 50 men. The march took almost two weeks. Every day she grew more and more tired, until she felt she could not go on. Every night she fell asleep in her clothes, like the rest of the soldiers.

One chilly, rainy afternoon the soldiers stopped to rest at a tavern. Deborah was warming herself at the fireplace. Suddenly she fainted and fell to the floor.

When she came to, her first thought was: "Have I been discovered?" Then she heard someone say, "What a pity such a young boy has to go to war."

Deborah breathed a sigh of relief. Her secret was still safe.

At West Point, she was given a uniform, a gun, and a heavy knapsack to carry on her back. She liked her uniform and the blue coat with its white buttons. She liked the new leather cap.

Every day she had to clean her gun and take part in the daily drill. She went on many raids against Tories. Soon she stopped thinking of war as an adventure.

War was the most horrible thing in the world, she thought. She heard the cries of men in pain. She saw them being shot down. She watched them die.

She had to go on long, long marches. Her shoes fell apart. Often she had to go without food for days. Sometimes she got so many blisters and sores on her hands she could hardly open or close her fingers.

But she never complained, and the other soldiers liked her for that. She did not drink or sing with the men, or take part in their wrestling contests or games. She tried to stay by herself as much as possible.

Everyone liked her. No one suspected that their quiet "Blooming Boy" was really a girl.

Deborah knew that her mother would worry about her if she did not hear from her. So she wrote a letter saying that she was fine. "I have found work in a large family," she wrote.

"Leave Me, I Am Going to Die!"

That winter, food was hard to get. The soldiers were always hungry. One day Deborah and a few soldiers rode their horses on a scouting party to a cave. The cave was filled with food that had been stolen by the Tories. The Tories planned to give it to the British soldiers.

There were jars of honey in the cave and butter, bacon, and cheese. Deborah and the other soldiers were filling their sacks when the Tories discovered them.

Quickly Deborah got up on her horse and galloped away. The enemy was close behind, firing their guns. Suddenly she felt something warm and wet run down her neck. She touched her neck. Her hand came away bloody.

Then she felt a sharp pain in her leg. Deborah said nothing but she knew that she had been shot. She slid off her horse. All of her strength was gone.

She could hardly take a step and she could not stand alone. She looked down

and saw that her boot was bloody. She had been shot in the leg too.

One of the soldiers stopped to help her. Deborah felt she would rather die than have him find out she was a woman.

"Leave me," she begged him. "Save yourself! I am going to die anyway!"

But the soldier took Deborah up on his horse and rode six miles to a hospital.

There, the doctor gave her wine to drink and bound up her head with a bandage. He gave her extra medicine and more bandages for her neck in case she should need them later.

Then he saw how pale she was and that she could hardly walk.

"Do you have any other wounds?" he asked, looking down at her boots.

"No," she said, her heart going like a cannon.

"Sit down, my young lad," said the doctor. "Your boot says you are lying."

Deborah knew she would have to act quickly. If he discovered she had been shot in the leg, he would make her take her clothes off so that he could remove the bullet. Then he would find out her secret.

"My head is throbbing with pain now," said Deborah. "Could I lie down for a while?"

The doctor led her to a small room. As soon as she was alone, she took out her pocket knife. She would use that knife and also the bandages and the medicine the doctor had given her.

She had to take that bullet out of her leg herself.

The first time she tried, she could not do it. She tried again. The pain was more than she could bear. But if she left the bullet for the doctor to remove, he would find out her secret. That thought gave her the courage to try once more.

This time, almost fainting from the

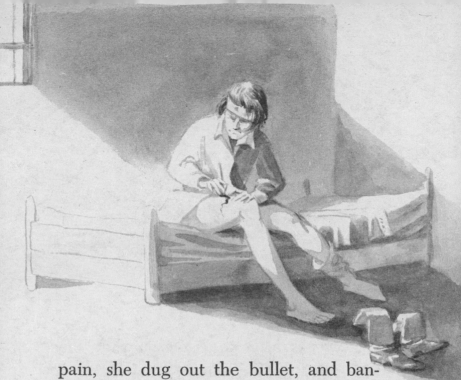

pain, she dug out the bullet, and bandaged her throbbing leg.

She rested as long as she could, but it was not long enough. The strongest soldier with the same wound would have been sent home and would not have to fight any longer.

No one knew how badly Deborah had been hurt. She didn't say a word to anyone.

Her leg never healed properly.

In a Cold Attic

Two weeks after she had been shot, she was called to take part in a march.

She started on the march. She was still weak and her leg throbbed with every step she took.

Richard Snow was another sick soldier. He was marching next to Deborah when he suddenly stumbled and fell to the ground.

He could not go on.

Deborah thought fast. She told the officer in charge of the march that she

would get Richard Snow to a nearby farmhouse. She said she would catch up with the others as soon as she could.

The officer agreed. This was Tory country. It was dangerous to stop and wait for one soldier to get better.

The nearest house belonged to a farmer named Van Tassel. He was not very friendly, but he led them up to his cold attic. "It's good enough for soldiers," he said.

Deborah's heart beat fast. "He must

be a Tory," she thought, "or a friend of Tories."

He was. Every night he gave noisy parties for his Tory friends.

Deborah's leg was feeling stronger day by day, but Richard Snow was growing weaker and sicker.

Deborah begged Van Tassel for a straw bed for the dying man.

"The floor is good enough for soldiers," he said.

One day Deborah heard footsteps on the stairs. Her heart jumped, but the voice of a girl made her breathe easier. It was Van Tassel's daughter.

She sneaked up food and water for Deborah and Richard.

But for Richard it was too late.

On the tenth day, he died. Van Tassel's daughter helped Deborah bury him.

Then Deborah set out to find the soldiers.

Discovery

General Paterson had heard of the quiet, brave soldier called Robert Shurtliff. On April 1, he chose Deborah to be his personal orderly. It was a high honor to serve him.

"I was given a good horse and fine equipment," she wrote. "I no longer slept on straw on the damp, cold ground, but on a good feather bed."

At last she could take off her dirty clothes and bathe in private.

In June she was sent to Philadelphia on an important mission. But it was not the time to be in the city. A terrible fever was spreading through Philadelphia. Many people got sick. Many died.

Deborah caught the fever too. One day she fainted and was put into a hospital bed. When she came to, she heard two men fighting over which of her clothes each one of them would take.

"Why, they think I'm dead!" Deborah thought in horror.

It took every bit of her strength to speak, to let the nurse know she was alive.

The nurse rushed to tell the doctor that Robert Shurtliff in bunk 5 whom they thought had died was still alive.

By the time Dr. Binney came, Deborah had sunk back into a coma.

The doctor examined her and discovered her secret!

Dr. Binney discovered that Robert Shurtliff, the young soldier, was really a young woman!

But he never made a single sign that he knew.

He introduced Deborah as Robert Shurtliff to his wife and daughters. He told them about the brave soldier who had had many adventures.

Deborah took walks through the city with Dr. Binney's family. Together they strolled through parks and gardens, went to the theater, and sailed on the Delaware River. She was invited to the fine houses of Philadelphia, still known only as a brave Continental soldier.

September was a good time to be in Philadelphia. The peace treaty had finally been signed in Paris. All Philadelphia was celebrating the end of the war. November 3 was the date set for the soldiers to be sent home to their families.

Deborah grew stronger in Philadelphia. Soon she was well enough to travel.

"Is It Really True?"

Dr. Binney gave her a letter to take back to General Paterson.

When Deborah arrived at the camp in early October, she found General Paterson alone.

She handed him Dr. Binney's letter. She was so afraid of what Dr. Binney had written to the General that she ran out of the room before the General could say a word.

An hour later, General Paterson sent for her.

Deborah was shaking like a leaf. He asked her to sit down. His voice was kind.

"Is it really true?" he said to her.

Her eyes filled with tears. For the first time as a soldier, she felt like sobbing and sobbing.

"What will be my fate, sir," she said, "if I say yes?"

"You have nothing to fear, Bobby — er, whoever you are," General Paterson said. "You have only my admiration and respect."

"Then God forbid that I should try and hide what you now know. Yes. It's true. I am Deborah Sampson."

The General shook his head. He could not believe this strange story.

"Can it really be so?"

"Sir, I have no desire to hide the truth any longer," Deborah said.

Then she thought of a plan and her eyes shone with mischief.

"Please sir, if you will get a dress for me — the fanciest gown you can find — you will see what Deborah Sampson can really look like."

The General did as he was asked.

And when Deborah next stood before him, she did not look anything like Robert Shurtliff, the soldier. She was dressed in a pink gown trimmed with lace and ribbons.

The General was amazed.

"Wait right here," the General cried.

"I'll call the captain. He has seen you every day so he should know you!"

When the captain came in, the General said, "We have a visitor whom you may know. This is Deborah Sampson."

"I should be proud to know her," said the captain, "but I don't."

The two men talked for a while. Then General Paterson asked, "Is there any news of my brave orderly — Robert Shurtliff?"

"I fear that he is dead," the captain said.

"The Revolution is full of miracles," General Paterson said. "And this young lady is one of them. Look at her closely and see if you do not see the face of Robert Shurtliff!"

The captain looked puzzled. *This lovely young lady in her pink gown? Robert Shurtliff, the young soldier?*

"You are making fun of me," the captain said.

"Sir," said Deborah. "I am who I am. Deborah Sampson and Robert Shurtliff. One and the same person."

She began to tell him all the names of the men in his company and about the adventures she had taken part in.

"That's enough," the captain said, shaking his head, "I must believe you now."

Deborah then told the two men why she had enlisted as a soldier and how she had kept her secret.

They took her out to the field where the rest of the soldiers were taking part in the daily drill. But not one man knew that the woman in the pink dress was Bobby, their soldier friend.

Deborah Sampson was discharged from the army on October 25, 1783. She had been in the army for about a year and a half. When she left she was given an excellent record of service.

A Farmer's Wife

That spring Deborah met Benjamin
Gannet, a farmer. Shortly after they
met they were wed. It was almost two
years from the day Deborah had signed
up for the army.

Deborah Sampson Gannet who had
been a soldier was now a farmer's wife.

Deborah's leg still hurt her. She could
not do heavy work around the farm.

Benjamin worked the farm hard and

well. They lived in a comfortable house. Roses and fruit trees flowered in the spring. A small stream flowed nearby.

It should have been a peaceful place for Deborah, after her many adventures.

But Deborah still longed for adventure. She still longed to travel — to know what was beyond the next hill.

Many people had heard about the good land in Ohio. They were moving out West — hundreds of them. Deborah wanted to take part in the move out West too.

"Let's go, Ben," she said to her husband.

He wanted to stay where he was. This land meant a great deal to him. He had worked it hard. He knew every rock, every tree on his land.

They did not go out West.

They stayed in Sharon, Massachusetts. They raised a family of three children — two girls and a boy. Then Deborah took in baby Susanna, whose mother had died. She raised Susanna as though she were her very own child.

Deborah was a gentle mother. She had seen enough of war to know that she hated fighting. Deborah's children grew up to be peaceful and kind.

Adventure Again

Deborah was 41 years old and still restless. Sometimes she taught in a school nearby. But that was not enough for her.

By then, her fame was well known. Her amazing story had begun to be told right after she got out of the army. Her adventures had been printed in a New York newspaper. They were told again in newspapers in Massachusetts.

Everyone wanted to know about Deborah's life as Robert Shurtliff, the soldier.

She gave her first talk in Sharon, her home town. It was a big success.

She decided to give talks in other places — cities like Boston, Providence, New York. Ben did not stop her. But he would not go with her. He would stay home with the children and work on the farm.

Deborah Sampson was one of the first women in this country to travel alone and give talks for money. She made all the travel arrangements and took care of every detail by herself.

She put notices in the local papers.

". . . Tickets may be had at the Court House from 5 o'clock till the performance begins. Price 25 cents, children half price. . . ."

She put on her old uniform and spoke about her adventures. She spoke against war. She told how she felt when she could not help the men around her who had been shot.

"I looked upon these scenes," she said,

"as one looks on a drowning man —
without being able to extend a hand."

She said she could not understand why
men fought. "My young mind wanted to
understand why man should rage against
his fellow man, to butcher or to be
butchered."

She kept a diary:

"May 5th, 1802: When I entered the
hall, I must say I was much pleased at
the appearance of the audience. It ap-
peared from almost every face that they
were full of unbelief — I mean in regard
to my being the person that served in
the Revolutionary Army."

She kept a record of the money she
had to pay out:

"Albany, August 31, 1802:

To old key keeper	2 00
To Mr. Barber for printing	3 00
To Mr. Lester for finding candles	1 34
To sweeping the court house	0 48

For cleaning the candle sticks 0 20
For brushing the seats 0 17
For the dressing of my hair 1 00
To boarding 6 00
To washing 1 34

Some of the money she earned she sent home. "I hope my family makes good use of it," she wrote.

Sometimes she made visits to her old army friends. Once she stayed at the home of old General Paterson and his wife.

But she began to miss her family more and more.

"O dear, could I but once more see my dear children," she wrote in her diary.

She was getting tired of traveling from one place to the next.

Besides, her leg still hurt her, especially when she was tired.

The next year she came home for good.

Two years later, in 1805, the government voted to give money to the soldiers who had been wounded in the war. Deborah received her share.

Thirteen years later, the government gave her more money. She got $8 a month until she died on April 29, 1827 at the age of 67.

More than a hundred years after she died, she was not forgotten. A warship was named after her.

Today, in Sharon, Massachusetts, the house she lived in with Ben and her children still stands. In the quiet cemetery, a marble tablet has been put up in her honor. Nearby is Deborah Sampson Street, named for the daring young woman who looked for adventure — and found it.